IMAGES
of America

EXETER

Parade onlookers on Water Street *c.* 1898. (EHS)

IMAGES
of America

EXETER

Carol Walker Aten

ARCADIA

First published 1996
Copyright © Carol Walker Aten, 1996

ISBN 0-7524-0291-9

Published by Arcadia Publishing,
an imprint of the Chalford Publishing Corporation
One Washington Center, Dover, New Hampshire 03820
Printed in Great Britain

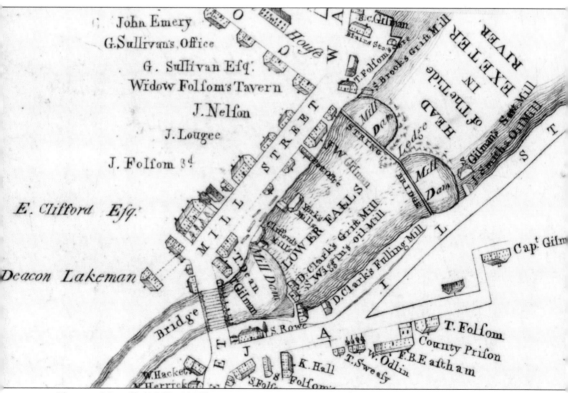

Phineas Merrill (1767–1815) was a surveyor, cartographer, and schoolmaster from Stratham who early on documented much of the seacoast area. He created two maps of Exeter dated 1802. (EHS)

Contents

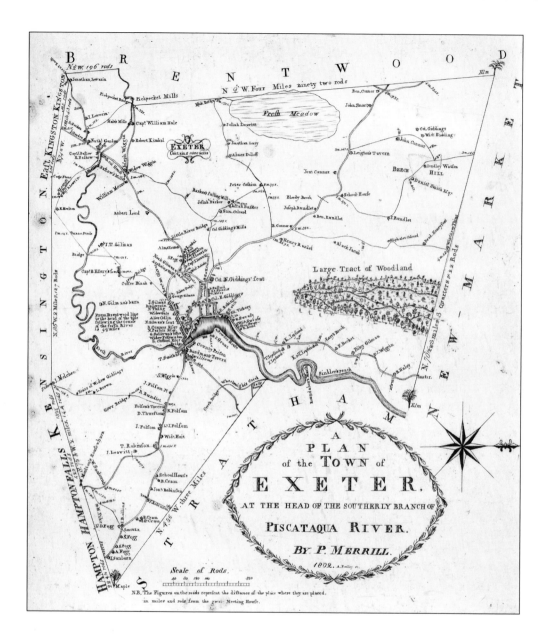

A
PLAN
of the TOWN of
EXETER,
AT THE HEAD OF THE SOUTHERLY BRANCH OF
PISCATAQUA RIVER.
BY P. MERRILL.
1802. A.Pratley sc.

Scale of Rods.

N.B. The Figures on the roads represent the distance of the place where they are placed, in miles and rods from the great Meeting House.

Introduction

Images of America: Exeter is a glimpse into Exeter's history between 1840 and 1920, a time when the town's economic growth was fueled by the river, mills, businesses, schools, and people in search of a quality of life that still remains. When looking for photographs to include in this book, there came a revelation that Exeter had changed very little, and tremendously. With a few glaring exceptions (such as the demolished Rockingham County Court House) and new construction, the town buildings, streets, and businesses still look very much the same as they did a century ago. Water Street is virtually unchanged, and ghosts of old shopkeepers and their trades linger inside a few businesses who have chosen to preserve the fine woodwork and old tin ceilings.

The Squamscott River no longer holds the same economic importance for the town as it once did—wharves, docks, and vessels of the last centuries live only in these photographs. Gone, too, are the horses and carriages—much of what is missing in Exeter was sacrificed to some requirement of the "new" automobile: either gas stations or parking spaces. The street trolley and the train had their heyday prior to the speed of modern car transport, and the beloved streetcars were eventually discontinued altogether. But the train, currently only a single track, shows a glimmer of revival in a proposed Portland to Boston run.

Exeter has always prized education; the growth of schools within the community reflects this. As early as the nineteenth century, Phillips Exeter Academy supported a diverse and international student population—a fact that is well-documented in the photographs within. Access to school learning was available to townspeople as early as the 1630s, and a secondary education system was in place by the mid-1800s. Team sports, fellowship, and student traditions continue, although most assuredly in different fashions.

But what has really changed are the people. Exeter's first immigrants came in 1638 from England via Massachusetts with Reverend John Wheelwright, eventually displacing the Native American Indians of the area—Squamscott Indians, a sub-tribe of the southern New Hampshire Penacooks and an Algonquian people. A second wave of immigrants followed, mostly British in origin, many of whom established the milling industries on the river or trades connected with the shipping industry. As some of these settlers established their own wealth, they accumulated enslaved people—fifty lived in town according to census records from 1767. By 1790, only two Africans remained enslaved; others had been freed and the African and black community in town remained steady at about eighty individuals until the 1860s.

As the mills expanded they attracted the next wave of immigrants, this time mainly from Europe and Canada. By the mid-1800s, Exeter was home to people speaking French (Canadian), Chinese, German, Gaelic, Polish, Russian, Italian, and Swedish, to name but a few. Exeter's blacks could read and write, but could not find meaningful work locally. The mill owners preferred to hire European immigrants, so Exeter's black population left in search of economic opportunities and social acceptance in larger New England cities. The European immigrants who came to Exeter between 1830 and 1880 had adult children born in New Hampshire who readily assimilated into the community, and whose families are here still. Exeter continues to attract immigrants—people looking for a good community to set down their own family roots—be they foreigners from as close as Massachusetts or as far away as Asia.

Carol Walker Aten, March 1996
In memory of my father, Robert E. Walker, another immigrant story.

One
The Squamscott and Exeter River

This *c.* 1857 image is the earliest known view of Exeter; it is an ambrotype copy of a daguerreotype. The sawmill building on String Bridge Island is on the far lower right. The center house is the home of John Lowe Jr. The last building on the right facing the river is the house of Stephen W. Dearborn. (DW)

Exeter Mills.

ONE REAM.

MANUFACTURED BY

FLAGG & WISWALL.

Paper was imported to New Hampshire until 1777 when the state's first paper mill was established in Exeter. This wood engraving by Henry Erastus Baldwin (1815–1855), printed by Oliver Smith of Exeter, depicts the Exeter Mills. Isaac Flagg operated a paper mill at the original Exeter site through the early nineteenth century, in partnership with Thomas, and later Otis, Wiswall. By 1870, the mill had burned twice; after the second time it was not rebuilt. (EHS)

The Falls at String Bridge are shown here in an 1860s stereoview by Exeter photographer William N. Hobbs (1830–1881). The first mill in town was built by Thomas Wilson at the foot of these falls for grinding grain in the 1650s. (DW)

In 1827 two companies formed to harness the water power of the river to manufacture cotton. The Exeter Mill and Water Power Company controlled the water power and conveyed it to the Exeter Manufacturing Company, which used the energy to operate its many spindles. This first brick mill was erected in 1830 and cotton sheetings were produced. This stereoview was taken by William N. Hobbs around the 1860s. (DW)

A photograph of the Exeter Manufacturing Company and String Bridge, c. 1882–84. It is a Thompson and Batchelder print. (EHS)

Wharves and businesses along the Squamscott River are shown here in a stereoview by William N. Hobbs. The prominent building in the distance is the Robinson Female Seminary, which dates this view to the late 1860s. (EHS)

Looking over Water Street to the Squamscott River in a stereoview by William N. Hobbs (c. 1875). The cellar hole was the initial site of St. Michael's Church, but this location was abandoned when the church was built on Center Street. (EHS)

The tidal Squamscott River looking toward the Swasey homestead, Fort Rock Farm, prior to the construction of Swasey Parkway around 1900. Note the wharves, docks, and schooner along the waterfront, vestiges of Exeter's early shipbuilding days. The following passage appeared in the June 18, 1860 issue of the *Exeter News-Letter*: "Port of Exeter: Arrived 14th inst., Sloop *Wild Cat*, Capt. Smith, Lumber, Slate, &c.—Also, Sloop *Harlequin*, Capt. Baker, Shingles, Laths, &c.—15th. Sloop *Sarah Quimby*, Capt. Fogg, Spruce Lumber. All of the above cargoes were for E.O. Lovering [shipyard owner]." (ENL)

An early 1900s view of the wharves along the Squamscott River in an advertising card from Exeter druggists Weeks & Seward. Ship and lumber yards stretched from the lower falls down to the end of Swasey Parkway, on the west side of the river. The last schooner from Exeter was launched in 1836. (EHS)

Once a familiar sight on the Squamscott River, the three-masted schooner *Lizzie J. Call* was built and launched in 1886. This view shows the vessel, owned by Henry W. Anderson, at work on the river at the turn of the century. (EHS)

The tug *Iva* towing the two-masted schooner *Ada J. Campbell* from Great Bay to Exeter, c. 1900. (EHS)

Gundalows were river craft that could carry heavy loads in shallow water and were designed to pass under bridges with their low profiles and adjustable masts. They were popular from the mid-eighteenth century through the nineteenth century. By the early twentieth century, they were being used as barges along the Squamscott River carrying coal, bricks and, as seen here, lumber. (EHS)

Possibly a view of the lumber yard at Henry W. Anderson's "Coal and Wood" business at 199 Water Street, c. 1900. (ENL)

Woodpiles at Anderson's coal and wood business at the edge of the Squamscott River, looking toward town, c. 1900. (ENL)

Dredging the Squamscott to build Swasey Parkway, *c.* 1927. Exeter Manufacturing Company mill buildings are visible across the water. (ENL)

An early-twentieth-century postcard depicts the "Fresh River [Exeter River] South from Greaney's Boathouse" on the left, looking toward Great Bridge.

Small inland mariners on the Exeter River, in a *c.* 1930s view of Great Bridge from Water Street to High Street. The first sawmills in Exeter were established near this bridge between 1647 and 1650 by Edward Gilman Jr. (PEA)

Two
Town Views

Retail businesses along Water Street are shown here in an early 1860s stereoview by William N. Hobbs. Hobbs was one of Exeter's most prolific early photographers. His first studio is pictured here on the second floor—the doorway is surrounded by portrait samples. (EHS)

A *carte de visite* of businesses along Water Street in 1860 photographed by Thomas E. Boutelle. (DW)

An elm-framed view of Water Street looking toward Great Bridge, from a Hobbs stereoview dated *c*. 1870. (EHS)

Water Street is shown here c. 1880s, in a photograph sold by Thompson and Batchelder. The town hall is visible on the left, and the spire in the distance is that of old St. Michael's Catholic Church, which is no longer extant. The building facades have hardly changed from the time this picture was taken a century ago. (PEA)

Mid-Water Street gussied up for a parade, *c.* 1900s. Note the trolley lines and tracks, and the granite hitch posts for carriages and horses. (PEA/ER)

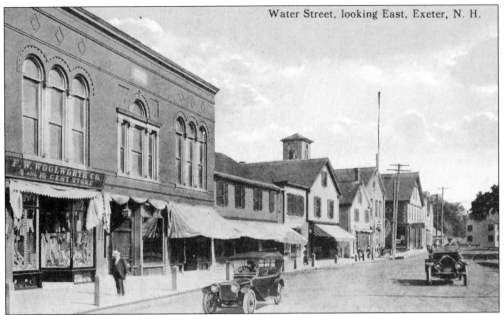

This postcard scene of Water Street was taken before 1915 when the IOKA Theater replaced the clapboard building directly next to the Masonic Block (where Woolworth's is depicted). The building with the cupola is the old fire station, the "Eagle Steamer House." (ENL)

This classic New England bandstand was a gift from Ambrose Swasey to the town in 1916, and replaced an earlier seasonal bandstand that had graced the same intersection of Water and Front Streets since the nineteenth century. The Exeter Brass Band has held concerts each summer in the bandstand since the group was founded in 1847. (ENL)

The Gilman Garrison is one of the town's earliest surviving structures and is now owned by the Society for the Preservation of New England Antiquities. The right ell, facing Water Street, housed a millinery shop run by Asenath Darling in the nineteenth century, and was later home to the Singer Sewing Machine Company.

This is an 1893 winter view of "The Square" at Water and Front Streets. On the right are the front steps of the town hall; in the distance the staging for the new Rockingham County Court House is visible. (EHS)

Designed by Arthur Gilman, the town hall (on the right) was erected in 1855. This *c.* 1896 view shows the original paint scheme of a reddish-brown sandstone color on the columns and trim. To the left is the completed Rockingham County Courthouse, conceived by architect George G. Adams. That building was razed in 1969 to provide a bank parking lot and drive-through facility. (EHS)

Designed by Ebenezer Clifford with Bradbury Johnson, the Tenney House was moved from its original site next to the town hall on Front Street in 1893 to make room for the new Rockingham County Court House. During its relocation to 65 High Street, the building's ell was moved by John Hallinan to River Street and became a two-story house; the barn (no longer extant) was moved to Linden Street by Lorenzo Nealey. This view is from around 1880. (EHS)

Exeter's First Congregational Church is shown here in a Hobbs stereoview, c. 1860s. This fourth meetinghouse of the church was built in 1798 from designs by Ebenezer Clifford and Bradbury Johnson. The interior was dramatically altered during an 1838 remodeling. (EHS)

In 1809 the Sullivan-Sleeper House was built for George Sullivan, lawyer and politician, at 4 Front Street. When the first Squamscott House was damaged by fire in 1871, this house was used as temporary quarters for the popular lodging until the hotel was rebuilt at the corner of Front and Court Streets. (EHS)

The Squamscott House was first established in 1837, and was rebuilt in 1851 after being destroyed by fire. In 1853, abolitionist politicians—led by Amos Tuck—met at the hotel and founded the Republican Party. In 1872 the Squamscott House was purchased by Phillips Exeter Academy for use as a dormitory and renamed Gorham Hall. The building served as the Squamscott House again from 1888 until around 1955, when it was converted to offices. (EHS)

Front Street is shown here in the 1880s, in a view looking toward the center of town. Under the elms to the right is the Nathaniel Gilman House, once the home of Governor Charles H. Bell. The building is now the property of Phillips Exeter Academy. This photograph was distributed by Thompson and Batchelder. (PEA)

The first Exeter Public Library was built in 1894 according to a design by architects Rotch and Tilden. In the entryway are four stone tablets engraved with the names of men who enlisted from Exeter to serve in the Civil War. The elegant classical revival structure now serves as the home of Exeter Historical Society.

Architect Ralph Adams Cram and Alfred Connor lay the cornerstone of the new Second Congregational Church on Front Street in 1897. Renamed Phillips Church a year later, it was not acquired by Phillips Exeter Academy until 1922. (PEA)

This winter view shows the completed Phillips Church at Tan Lane and Front Street. (PEA)

This impressive Second Empire-style home was originally a smaller colonial structure built for the Reverend Isaac Hurd around 1820. During the 1860s, architect Rufus Sargent remodeled the house extensively for Benjamin L. Merrill, and it became known as the Hurd-Merrill-Isley House at 48 Front Street. The house was razed in 1939. (EHS)

Demolished around 1930, the Chadwick House once stood where the Exeter Inn on Front Street is now located. Once a two-story house, the structure acquired three floors when Captain John Chadwick raised it off the ground and then built an additional story underneath. Frances Rogers Chadwick (Mrs. John Chadwick), her granddaughter Hazel Chadwick (standing patiently next to her nurse), and Annie Chadwick are depicted here. (EHS)

Traffic in the 1890s spins down Front Street and past the gate to the Robinson Female Seminary and principal's residence. The image is a glass plate negative print by Albert C. Buzell. (EHS)

Looking up "Town Hill"—Main Street and the fork at right to Water Street, *c.* 1860s. (DW)

31

A *c.* 1870s view of Giddinges Tavern, built in the early seventeenth century on the corner of Park and Summer Streets. Zebulon Giddinges operated an inn here until his death in 1789. Park Street at that time served as a "mast way"—a road upon which lumbermen hauled their felled timber to the Squamscott River. It was here that participants in the "Mast Tree Riot" of 1734 assembled to don their Native American disguises before an illegal protest. (EHS)

This photograph by the Currier Studio shows the rear of the Robinson House on Main Street. The paneling in the house was saved and much was reused in the Tilton House at 72 Front Street during a 1930–31 restoration. The workman was also employed in the construction of the Jeremiah Smith Hall administrative building at nearby Phillips Exeter Academy. (PEA)

The north side of Tan Lane is shown here, c. 1893. Tan Lane was the busy site of several eighteenth and nineteenth-century tanneries that produced the leather for saddles, shoes, harnesses, carriages, etc. (PEA)

Laying the steam mains in 1908. Trenches were dug behind the old academy boiler house off Spring Street. (PEA)

This is the Ladd-Gilman House around 1860, in a Hobbs stereoview. First begun by Nathaniel Ladd around 1721, the house was expanded in 1738 and again in 1752 by Daniel Gilman. Daniel gave the house to his son, Nicholas Gilman Sr., a shipbuilder, merchant, and the first state treasurer. In 1783, John Taylor Gilman inherited the house; he served as state treasurer and in 1794 became governor of New Hampshire. His brother, Nicholas Jr., and John Langdon were the two New Hampshire delegates to the Constitutional Convention in Philadelphia in 1787.

Exeter N H Cincinnati Memorial Hall

In 1904, the Society of Cincinnati in the State of New Hampshire purchased the property and made alterations to the Ladd-Gilman House. Society members, descendants of the officers of the Continental Army of the American Revolution, developed a military museum and meeting place there over the next eighty years. The property, which included the first state treasury, became one of the first historic houses in the nation open to the public. The house is now part of the American Independence Museum.

Built in 1875 on Center Street with the parsonage next door, facing Water Street, St. Michael's Catholic Church was demolished in 1959 when a new church was erected on Front Street. The Gothic Revival brick building was designed by John P. Heffernan and was a typical example of American church architecture of the time. This postcard dates prior to 1904.

The Opera House, shown here *c.* 1910. The First Baptist Church was established in 1800 and built in 1805 on Spring Street. The congregation's second building, on the corner of Spring and Water Streets, was used as a house of worship from 1833 until 1875. In 1876 the structure was used as an armory until it was converted by James D.P. Wingate, owner-editor of the *Gazette*, to the Opera House. The opening performance at the Opera House coincided with the celebration of Exeter's 250th anniversary in 1888. The first moving pictures in town were shown at the Opera House on May 18 and 19, 1903, by the London Bioscope Company. The IOKA Theater began construction in April 1915. It eventually replaced the Opera House after the latter burned in September 1919 and was then demolished. (EHS)

The Moses-Kent House was designed by Rufus Sargent for Deacon Henry C. Moses in 1868. The house, which stands at One Pine Street, was later occupied by George Kent, owner of the Exeter Cotton Mill. This view is dated February 1923. (EHS)

The Josiah Coffin Smith House, *c.* 1870, on Gilman Lane near High Street, is now the property of Phillips Exeter Academy. (ENL)

This turn-of-the-century photograph shows the gambrel-roofed Odiorne-Bickford House on 25 Cass Street, which is thought to have been constructed in 1737 by Colonel John Gilman, for his son, Major John Gilman. (EHS)

A view looking toward the intersection of Portsmouth Avenue and High Street around 1900. The white houses on each corner of the intersection were removed to make room for gas stations. The elm trees, prominent in most of the early views of Exeter, were lost to disease in the 1930s. (ENL)

The sprawling Portsmouth Avenue farmstead of the Cunningham family is captured in a glass plate negative from the early twentieth century by Edwin L. Cunningham. The now busy commercial road was once bordered by farms and homesteads such as this, all of which have been lost to strip malls, fast-food restaurants, and gas stations. (EHS)

This *c.* 1890 photograph of the Kimball Farm on Pickpocket Road depicts rustic properties on the outskirts of Exeter. Many such areas are now the sites of housing developments. (EHS)

This brick commercial structure was built in 1860 by Kelly, Gardner, and Thompson to replace a previous building that had burned. G.C. Lyford sold fabrics, clothing, and other dry goods at this location. Robert C. Thomson relocated his tailor business here after being burned out of his old shop in March 1860. Attorney Frances O. French had an office on the upper floor, as did Amos Tuck. By March 1861, Mr. French had married Mr. Tuck's youngest daughter, Ellen, and a new sign, "Tuck & French," was hung announcing the partnership of French with his father-in-law. (EHS)

Three
Livelihoods and Trades

Rowell & James was one of the many grocers in business on Water Street, *c.* 1870. (EHS)

Collishaw & Page were "Dealers in fine groceries, canned goods, flour & provisions" at 5 Water Street, c. 1905. (EHS)

Exeter residents could shop from a wide variety of grocers and dealers in dry goods, fancy goods, and provisions. Teas, coffees, spices, canned goods, fruits, vegetables, table condiments, flour, and grain were all staple foods and readily available. The town had as many as twenty providers of such goods in the 1880s and early 1900s, including Herbert F. Dunn, Porritt & Carr, S.W. Langley, George L. Swain, and Poggio & Gaiero. (PS)

Local shops sold candy, flour, potatoes, and various bottled and canned goods. In the 1901 town directory, four businesses were listed as sellers of "Fruit, Confectionery & Tobacco"—Frank Ciocca, Charles A. Lamprey, Margie Bros., and Rockingham Fruit Co. All of these businesses were located on Water Street. (PS)

The following passage appeared in the April 27, 1900 issue of the *Exeter News-Letter*: "C.C. Russell & Co. received a wagon, the New Beverly of Amesbury, made last week which is attracting much attention. It is built for light delivery work and order taking and also pleasure driving. It is a very handsome and stylish wagon." (EHS)

This structure on Water Street, adjacent to the town hall, housed the American Express Company run by Charles F. Hervey, and the Goodwin Brothers grocery store. It was replaced in 1959 by a bank parking lot. (EHS)

This is the interior of Goodwin's grocery store. (EHS)

According to an advertisement in the 1915–17 Exeter Town Directory: "To trade with W.P. Bartlett & Co. is to insure the most careful selection of all that goes on your table—and the most painstaking service in the filling of your order." (EHS)

A.S. Wetherell, druggist, was in Janvrin's Block on Water Street before 1888. "The largest and best selected stock of pure, fresh drugs & medicines in town. Prescriptions accurately prepared by experienced persons. Best Soda & Vichy waters. Rich Fancy goods, cutlery, pocket books, toilet cases, Meerschaum goods, soaps, perfumes, colognes, etc. Christmas cards in great variety, Patent medicines, Foreign Trusses, supporters and shoulder braces, of every kind." (EHS)

This c. 1900 photograph of the interior of Weeks and Seward's well-appointed drugstore was taken by southern Maine photographer J.S. Mitchell. The original wood pharmaceutical cabinetry, now part of Carrier Family Jewelers, is today's only surviving remnant of Exeter's old drugstores. (PEA)

In 1898 the Exeter Drug Company, whose shop window is depicted here, c. 1905, became the first Exeter business to install electricity. Located at 147 Water Street, the drugstore was one of many that flourished in town during the turn of the century. (PS)

The Carlisle Building on Water Street was constructed in 1875. It housed Phillips Exeter Academy's gymnasium on the first floor, and a photography studio on the second floor was occupied in turn by William N. Hobbs (1880s), J. Bela Robinson (1872–1883), Samuel G. Morse (1883–1894), R.E. Field (1894–1895), Folsom & Carlisle (1895–1897), H. Lewis Nye (1897–1898), and E.F. Fuller (c. 1898). Portraits around the doorway advertise the business upstairs. (PEA)

The Burlingame Block was built in 1874 on Water Street. Notice the workman on top of the roof. The Odd Fellows met on the second floor and Thompson and Batchelder ran their book and stationery businesses downstairs. (PEA/ER)

The first telephone company in Exeter was established in the basement of the Burlingame Block around 1882, with Maggie A. Noonan as operator. The New England Telephone Company office, pictured here around 1910, was merged with the Exeter Telephone Company about this time. The conglomerate became known as the New England Telephone and Telegraph Company. (EHS)

Charles Folsom is shown here c. 1880. Folsom's Oyster House was established in 1868 on Water Street, in the former home of Exeter's silversmith and first postmaster, John Ward Gilman. In 1896 Folsom tore the old business down and constructed the brick block known as the Masonic Block, which featured three stores on the first floor and the Masonic Hall above. (EHS)

John H. Elkins & Co., Meats & Provisions, was located on Water Street where the IOKA Theater now stands, *c.* 1892. (EHS)

"There are a great many meat markets in this section of the State and they are well patronized as a rule, for the Americans as a nation are great meat-eaters, and fortunately have the means to gratify their fondness for flesh food. [One shop's] premises covers an area of some 1200 square feet, and contains desirable stock comprising meats and provisions of all kinds, as well as fresh fish in great variety. . . . All classes of trade are catered to, and the most fastidious purchasers will find goods here that will give entire satisfaction. . . ." This passage originally appeared in *Leading Businessmen of Exeter* (Boston: Mercantile Publishing Co., 1891). (PS)

Between the 1880s and early 1900s, Exeter supported several types of merchants who provided clothing and goods to their customers. "Dressmakers" were often ladies who prepared custom garments in their homes for female clients; Nellie Smart, on Elm Street, was one such clothier. "Merchant tailors," likewise, were men who created custom-made suits for their male customers; Mr. S. Lewis on Water Street began such a business in 1889. The concept of "ready-made" clothing was also well-established at this time, and many preferred shopping from an open stock of goods, such as that depicted in this shop interior. (PS)

"Clothing and Mens Furnishings" were found at businesses such as H.P. Robinson's in Wood's Block, The Boston Clothing House, and A.S. French's on Water Street. French's sold "Clothing, Hats, Caps and Gents Furnishings, Trunks, Bags and Rubber Goods," and according to *Leading Businessmen of Exeter*: ". . .Mr. French carries so large an assortment of sizes so as to be able to fit men, youths, or boys, in a perfectly satisfactory manner, and if you want a suit made to order you can select your material from a large stock of fresh samples, and obtain a suit in quality of stock, work, fit, or price equal to that you would obtain [in] Boston." (PS)

Exeter could well be considered a major "shoe town." Major factories such as Gale Brothers and the Exeter Boot & Shoe Company employed hundreds of local and immigrant workers as shoemakers, lasters, cutters, and trimmers. The town also supported several shoe shops and, as depicted here, four cobblers around 1901: Peter Blake, William Booth, George W. Gadd, and Frank L. Graves. (PS)

The 1901 town directory lists Cornelia Bush as a bootblack. Since the town's mill owners tended to discriminate against blacks in hiring, many not engaged in menial labor were self-employed as barbers, bootblacks, or housekeepers. Between 1880 and 1910, Exeter census records list blacks employed as laborers, janitors, barbers, stonemasons, house servants, and laundresses. (PS)

This is the interior of O.H. Sleeper's "diamonds, watches, clocks, silverware, jewelry, novelties, spectacles, eyeglasses" store, c. 1900–1905. The shop was established in 1883 on Front Street, near the corner of Water Street, and according to *Leading Businessmen of Exeter*: "The market is so flooded nowadays with cheap and worthless watches got up expressly to 'sell' that it is necessary to use considerable care in the selection of a time-piece, as otherwise one is liable to be badly taken in. Of course this danger can be entirely avoided by dealing with a reputable house . . . and in this connection we may be excused for calling to attention of our readers to the goods handled by Mr. O.H. Sleeper, for his stock is a most carefully chosen one, and contains reliable articles exclusively." (PS)

Charles G. Sheldon operated a "jeweler and optician" business on Center Street, and Walter E. Burtt had a long-standing jewelry store at 189 Water Street. The shop interior depicted here reflects the type of business that competed with O.H. Sleeper's larger operation on Front Street. (PS)

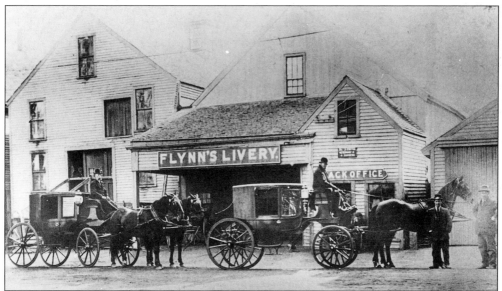

Jerry Flynn's livery stable on Court Street was located behind the Squamscott House, c. 1901. The man driving the front hack is Tom Campbell. The shorter man standing is "Pete" Bean (hack driver), and next to him is Jerry Flynn. The livery was demolished in 1927 and replaced by a garage, making the necessary transition from horse power to gas power as automobiles became popular. (EHS)

This commercial kitchen was photographed *c*. 1900-05. By 1901 Exeter had seven restaurants and three hotels: the Hotel Lincoln on 75 Main Street, the Squamscott House at Front and Court Streets, and the American House on 36 Water Street. The latter was recorded in *Leading Businessmen of Exeter* as: ". . .A thoroughly well-kept hotel. The table is excellent, the service prompt and obliging, and the terms are moderate. . .There is a first class livery and boarding stable connected, where excellent teams may be obtained at very short notice. . .and as the country adjacent abounds with beautiful drives. . . The house has many attractions and can accommodate fifty guests. Employment is given to six capable assistants, and every effort is made to give all attention necessary for the comfort of all guests." (PS)

The A. Merrill & Sons store and house at the corner of Spring Street and "Town Hill" (Main Street) is no longer standing. The 1872 town directory advertised "Hats, Caps and Furs—wool pullers, and dealers in native & foreign wool & wool skins. Also all kinds of shipping furs." (EHS)

Fur trading was still a vital business in New Hampshire during the nineteenth century, as evidenced by this hunter/merchant with his pelts. (PEA/ER)

The Folsom Tavern was built around 1775 by Colonel Samuel Folsom, brother of General Nathaniel Folsom. Revolutionary officers met there on Tuesday, November 18, 1783, and formed the Society of the Cincinnati in the State of New Hampshire. George Washington stopped by on the morning of November 4, 1789, "to partake of a collation" (breakfast) during his presidential tour of New England. This *c.* 1860 photograph shows the tavern on its original site.

Water Street was widened in 1869 to alleviate the traffic congestion in the center of town, and the Folsom Tavern was set back on a high foundation. This allowed for the construction of shops, as well as a passenger waiting room for the Exeter, Hampton, and Amesbury Street Railway (the "trolley") on the lower floor.

Oliver R. Yeaton and his wife, Augusta Cenith Beardslee, came from Lynn, MA, about 1906 to run the waiting station at the Folsom Tavern, and opened a restaurant. They lived upstairs in the tavern for a time and their children George, Carl, Leon, and Nellie worked with them. The station was a very busy stop on the trolley line, since it provided people a way to get to the beach. Tickets were sold, along with cigars, confections, and homemade lunches. By 1929 the prime corner lot was sold to the Standard Oil Company as the site for a gas station. The historic tavern was moved over the course of four days down Water Street to its current site on Spring Street. It is now part of the American Independence Museum.

Harold McKeen waits behind the restaurant counter.

Luke Leighton ran a cigar and tobacco store at 62 Water Street around 1900. Cigar and tobacco businesses were often established as part of pool halls or bowling alleys throughout New England. (PS)

A large number of hairdressers and barbers earned a living at the turn of the century in Exeter. Customers could choose the convenience of small businesses or the social atmosphere of larger establishments, such as the one shown here. Over eleven salons were set up on Lincoln, Water, Front, and Pleasant Streets, and stylist Fred Rabador served the patrons of the Squamscott House. (PS)

This driver and horse-drawn wagon of the G.C. Lumber & Box Company, at Rockingham and Winter Streets, posed for a photograph, *c.* 1907–10. George Clement Colburn lived at 35 Pine Street with his wife Elizabeth, and two sons, Dwight and George Clement Jr. (EHS)

Around 1890 Union Street had several businesses, including the Button Brothers Bakery. Depicted here from left to right are: William Ross Button, John Ross Button, and Christian Stanger Ross. The bakery was established around the same year as this photograph, and by 1903 was operated solely by John Ross Button. (EHS)

In 1905, the Exeter Post Office staff was busy processing the latest rage—picture postcards. James H. Batchelder added local views of Exeter to his large selection of souvenir postcards, and Frank W. Swallow began his postcard business. The "Swallow Girls" hand-tinted the postcards at 40 Lincoln Street, the residence of Lucy Boswell, one of the artists. From left to right are: (front row) Fred Sanborn, Frank Vickery, Herbert Hiscook, Postmaster George Stokell Jr., Mary Eliot, George Higgins, and Harry Prescott; (back row) Charles Stackpole, Charles Gilmore, Bert Scott, Rupert Ford, Edward Chase, Roy Burpee, and Arthur Vaughn. (EHS)

The serious crew of the Exeter Lumber Company on Winter Street, owned by Frank W. Parker and L.E. Webster, posed for this photograph around 1910. (EHS)

The Rubber Step Manufacturing Company was brought to Lincoln Street in 1892 by Daniel Gilman. The company, which originally manufactured carriage steps and car treads, began producing and repairing tires as the automobile gained popularity. It also produced non-skid rubber soles and heels for shoes. In 1916, a year after this picture was taken, the manufacturing plant became the Stearns Rubber Company; two years later it was sold again to the Samuel Butler & Company of Boston. By 1923 the building housed the Turner Asbestos Company. (EHS)

Exeter always had at least a half-dozen blacksmiths prior to the days of automobiles. Between 1900 and 1905, horseshoes, tools, and metalwork were being forged by: A.J. Fogg, 8 South Street; George W. and John Green, Court Street; Fred W. Kent, the River Street "horse shoer"; George P. Lane, 221 Water Street; the Safford Brothers, 30 Park Street; Albert M. Vroom, Court Street; Olaf Hanson, String Bridge Island; and Jared P. Whitcomb at the rear of 11 Water Street. (PS)

This barn, located in a field that ran from Front Street to Brentwood Road, belonged to Benjamin L. Merrill. This rural view of in-town Exeter is startling today. The cart path, seen in this Samuel G. Morse photograph of July 13, 1888, was later upgraded to Washington Street. (EHS)

The Exeter Manufacturing Company started textile production in 1830 in mills at the Exeter Falls. A large steam boiler was shipped via the B & M Railroad and hauled by seven horses back to the mill to be installed. (EHS)

The Exeter Water Works sent a water sprinkler around each summer to help contain the dusty roads. The sprinkler is shown here passing the town hall in a c. 1894–95 photographed by R.E. Field . (EHS)

Exeter's first commercial water supply took the form of the "Exeter Aqueduct." The aqueduct, first used in 1801, brought water to the village through hollow logs from springs near Lincoln Street. The Exeter Water Works Company was in operation by October 1886, working to improve Exeter's water quality. The reservoirs and pumps were established on a small stream leading to Wheelwrights Creek, and the water was driven to a stand pipe on the summit of Prospect Hill. The above image is a 1900 photograph of the steam pumps; below is an exterior view of the plant on Portsmouth Avenue. (EHS)

When the Boston & Maine reached Exeter in 1840, the railroad consisted of a single track with sidings. The town's population of 2,913 wasn't thrilled with the idea of progress. Alfred R. Wightman, in "The Railroad Comes to Exeter" (Exeter Historical Society Bulletin 6, 1949), states: "Opposition to the railroads was on two grounds: first, the locomotive was something strange. . . . It upset one's way of life. It was an innovation. . . . It was a menace. . . . Second, the laying of tracks across one's land was regarded as an invasion of property rights . . ." This photograph of the train station on Lincoln Street is from around 1890, after the town had adjusted to the convenience of rail service. (EHS)

The first train station on Lincoln Street, pictured here in a stereoview by William N. Hobbs, was built in 1860. The Italianate brick building was a national style popular through the Civil War period. C.C. Littlefield and his family ran a popular restaurant at the old depot. (EHS)

The first depot (shown above) was destroyed by fire, and a new station (shown below) was built in 1890–91 at the same location on Lincoln Street by the Damon Brothers, architects from Haverhill, MA. The new building, which still stands, was designed in a vernacular Romanesque style made famous by Henry H. Richardson during the late nineteenth century. (EHS)

The Exeter Street Railway Company was incorporated in 1889, but the line was not constructed until 1897 due to a lack of financing. Judge Charles M. Lamorey drove the first spike into the rail near the Whittier Hotel in Hampton on May 19, 1897. (EHS)

"The first rail of the Exeter, Hampton & Amesbury Street Railway was laid May 19, 1897; the first car ran over its tracks July 3, 1897 and opened up to Exeter and New England one of the most attractive beaches on the Atlantic Coast, Hampton Beach. . . . Not only has this road been the means of building up Hampton Beach to an incredible extent but it has been the vehicle by which thousands of tourists have visited the elm-shaded streets of Exeter." This passage originally appeared in *Exeter: The Business Center of Rockingham County* (1910). (PEA)

The Rockingham Electric Company was formed in 1897. The business was founded expressly to purchase electricity from the Exeter & Hampton Street Railway and sell it to the towns of Exeter and Hampton. A state charter forbade the railway company to directly sell the electricity, thus forcing the creation of the separate electric company. (EHS)

William B. Burlingame started a bicycle business at his home on Linden Street in response to the development of the safety bicycle in 1874. The Rambler was one of the most expensive models at $125. In 1895, about the time this photograph was taken, 10 percent of the townspeople owned a bicycle. (EHS)

Four

People of Exeter

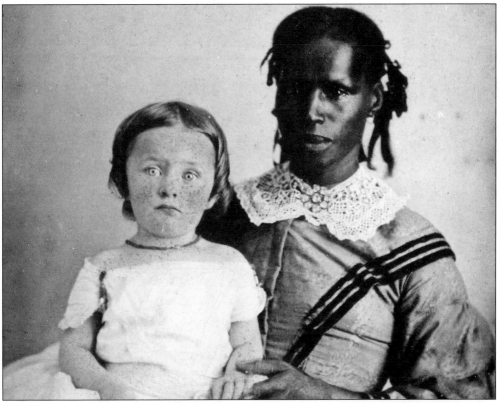

This daguerreotype of Lillian Walker and her nurse was taken around 1853–54. Lillian's father was John Moses, deacon of the First Baptist Church in Exeter. With his second wife, Dora Moses Walker, and five of their twelve children, the Moses family moved to Tennessee and established a Baptist church there. Dora and the children returned to Exeter during the Civil War, and Lillian Walker remained. She graduated from the Robinson Female Seminary in 1875 and married Rufus Walker Williams. (EHS)

The following photographs were taken by several of the many photographers who worked in or traveled through Exeter after the advent of photography in 1839 by Louis Daguerre and William Talbot. Early photographers often advertised in the *Exeter News-Letter*, and by doing so, attracted many customers to the new-fangled and affordable way of capturing their likenesses.

Left:: A *carte de visite* of a young man by Thomas E. Boutelle, *c.* 1850–59. Boutelle had several studios during his business in Exeter, including one on String Bridge Island that burned in March 1860. (DW)

Below left: A young boy in coat around 1850–60 in a *carte de visite* by the Davis Brothers at 40 Water Street. (EW)

Below right: A pouting boy in a tintype from 'Davis Brothers' Ambrotype and Photograph Rooms, No. 40 Water Street, *c.* 1860. Davis Brothers eventually sold their business to their apprentice, William N. Hobbs. (DW)

Above left: A Gentleman smoking a cigar in a ruby glass ambrotype from "R.A. Reed's 25 cent Ambrotype Saloon, on Clifford Street, near Water Street," *c.* 1860. (DW)
Above right: A *carte de visite* of a woman's head by J.A. Farham, *c.* 1870s. (EW)
Below left: A *carte de visite* of a man with a mustache by "Chick," another photographer traveling through Exeter, *c.* 1870–80. (EW)
Below right: An 1870s photograph of a young girl, taken by J. Bela Robinson, who began working with William N. Hobbs *c.* 1872, and photographed actively until around 1883. (EW)

This *c.* 1875–81 *carte de visite* of a young woman is by William N. Hobbs, one of Exeter's most prolific and important early photographers. He bought out the Davis Brothers in 1865 after working with them for about five years. From 1871 to 1875, he worked at 40 Water Street in their former studio. By 1876 he had moved to 64 Water Street, and by the time of his death in 1881 he had moved to 94 Water Street. (EW)

A stereoview of people in an unidentified forest, possibly Gilman Park, created by local photographer William N. Hobbs, *c.* 1860s. (EHS)

The Exeter Cornet Band is shown here in front of town hall on the band's 20th anniversary. From left to right are: (front row) "Old" Robinson (band leader), Lou Rundlett, George Tilton, Ben Ellison, and Bruce Brigham; (middle row) unidentified, unidentified, James Carlisle, Ed Tilton, and Charles Walker; (back row) unidentified, John Leavitt, Lou Harvey, Perry Tilton, Gus Towle, and J. Warren Tilton. (ENL)

The Exeter Cornet Band leads a parade on Front Street in front of the Gardner House, c. 1870. (ENL)

On the reverse of this intriguing portrait of one of Exeter's most noted homeless citizens is an inscription by R.D. Sawyer: " 'King David' —David George—A harmless old fellow touched in the head over religion called himself King David, but was confused a bit for he wore a 'coat of many colors.'[after Joseph.] He traveled about, talked religion & stayed where they [would] keep him & sold his photo. Newell Nealey [an Exeter photographer] used to let him stay 2 or 3 days—he walked with stately dignity & used a staff & had bright colored ribbon & bits of cloth sewed on his clothes—his period 1875–1885." This photograph was taken by A.J. Whittemore, Rochester. (EHS)

This *c.* 1870s photograph, taken by William N. Hobbs, shows an unexplained gathering. From left to right are: (front row) Ellen Moulton, Judge Shute, Lillie Smith (Tillie's sister), Jonathan Wood, and Georgia Shute; (back row) Charles Byington, Amelia Weeks (Judge Henry Shute's first wife), Frances Moulton, Will Folsom, Tillie Smith, and Charles Wingate. (EHS)

Reverend Israel F. Otis and his wife, Olive Osgood Otis, were photographed by Samuel G. Morse about 1880. The couple moved to their home at 79 Front Street in the 1860s. (EHS)

Charles E.L. Wingate is shown here with his mother (Arianna Mitchell Wingate Lovering), his wife, and children, around 1887. (EHS)

Participants in the "Old Folks Concert," c. 1888–89, included, from left to right: (front row) Albertus T. Dudley, Annie Dow, Florence Dow, and unidentified; (middle row) Miss Rice, Mrs. C. Knight, Dr. Alice Chesley, Mrs. Samuel G. Morse, and Helen Anderson; (back row) Jonathan Taylor, Ned Shute, Professor Stetson, Harry Shute, and Mrs. John Taylor. (EHS)

"The Summer of 1889," featuring academy instructors, students, and local residents. Included in this picture are George White, Mrs. W.A. Francis, Florence Wood, Mr. Stetson, William Gale, Nellie Kelly, Nora Hatch, Sue Thompson, Harold N. Fowler, Helen Bell, Annie Chadwick, Grace Scammon, Maud Fowler, Helen Dutch (Anderson), Albertus T. Dudley, and Mr. Stone. (EHS)

Albert Clark Buzell (1844–1910) relaxing in Gilman Park, in what may be a self-portrait, c. 1890. Buzell graduated from Phillips Exeter Academy in 1861, and attended Harvard and Harvard Law School until 1868. After a few years of practicing law in Boston, he opened an office in Exeter. His passions included books, music, and photography, and he produced glass plate negatives at his home at 86 Front Street. (EHS)

Mary and Stafford Allen Francis are shown here sledding in the snow about 1891. The children's father, William A. Francis, was a math instructor at Phillips Exeter Academy from 1892 until the early 1910s. Stafford attended the academy, graduating in 1906. (EHS)

This c. 1890 photograph includes Miss Ellen Wentworth, Mrs. John Perry, Miss Mary Gordon, and Miss Eliza U. Bell (standing). Miss Bell was the first clerk at the new Exeter Cottage Hospital in 1892. Miss Wentworth lived at the corner of Front and Lincoln Streets. Mrs. Perry's husband, John, was a journalist and they lived at the Ladd-Gilman House. Miss Gordon was the daughter of Nathaniel Gordon. (EHS)

Exeter businessman Daniel Gilman pose with his wife, children, and sister-in-law Roberta Crawford of Nashville, TN. Gilman donated 10 acres of land at the confluence of the Exeter and Little Rivers to the town in 1890. The area was named Gilman Park. (EHS)

Clarence Getchell (standing on the right) graduated from Phillips Exeter Academy in 1879 and Harvard in 1883. He taught physics and chemistry until 1888 and later worked in his family's stove and hardware business, Getchell & Taylor. He was one of Exeter's selectmen in 1908. (EHS)

A c. 1890s photograph of skeet shooting on Jady Hill. The Exeter Gun Club was founded in 1878 and was the second trap shooting club founded in the world. (ENL)

The occasion that prompted the creation of this cheering section, *c.* 1895, remains a mystery. (EHS)

A portrait of Charles Treadwell, created by E.F. Fuller Studios at 94 Water Street, *c.* 1897. Treadwell was a local farmer who lived at 135 High Street. (EHS)

On June 10, 1897, the Boston-bound rail freight No. 600 derailed. The accident was caused by the washout of the culvert behind J. Osgood Marsh's residence on Newmarket Road. Three men were killed—engineer Charles Rankin, brakemen Elna M. Chandler, and Asa Young. Fireman Daniel King was taken to the newly opened Exeter Cottage Hospital with severe injuries. Brakeman Edward Clark and conductor Eugene Thurston escaped injury in the caboose. (EHS)

Horsemen ride over String Bridge during a parade around 1898. (EHS)

The famed Exeter Hand Pump, shown here in 1898, is the property of the town's fire department and part of its collection of historic fire-fighting equipment. The hand pump was a great improvement over the town's original fire-fighting methods, which involved hurling leather buckets full of water at fiery targets. (EHS)

The Exeter Fire Department pose at the Central Fire Station on Court Street, c. 1900–15. The grand station was later horizontally severed in half and then refaced. The building now serves as the town's senior citizen center. (ENL)

Local students hang-out at one of Exeter's drugstore soda fountains on Water Street, around 1900. (PS)

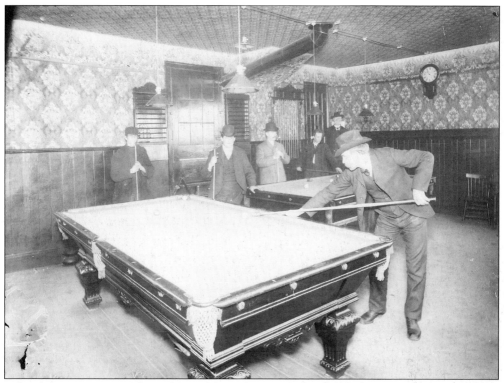

Billiards rooms were popular gathering places for townsmen at the turn of the century. Henry J. Eno ran Exeter's primary pool spot at 163 Front Street. (PS)

Shooting gallerys such as this one were present in many towns of the same period. The saw blades in the background were used to stop bullets aimed for the duck decoys below. The mask of a black man appears at the center of the ball target, indicating plainly the social prejudices that were present throughout New England. (PS)

Police Superintendent Charles G. Gooch (seated) poses with his two of his eight officers, William H. Hamilton and C. Fred Fifield, c. 1900. The police station was located in the first floor of the town hall. In the 1900 town report, it was noted that there were 162 arrests for the year: 156 male offenders and 6 female. There were "5 assaults, 1 breaking and entering, 1 breaking glass, 106 drunk, 2 disorderly conduct, 2 embezzlements, 1 insane person taken to the asylum, 27 keeping for sale, 7 larceny, 1 refusing to move on the street when asked, 1 snaring partridges, 1 selling without license, 1 shooting dog, 2 threatening, and 1 using profane language." (PS)

This picnic in the woods possibly occurred in Gilman Park. The image was taken by an Exeter photographer around 1900. (PEA/ER)

In 1765, men who took part in the Boston Tea Party formed a society known as the Sons of Liberty. After the Revolutionary War, this society merged with other patriotic groups to form a new organization named "The Order of the Red Men." It became a popular fraternal and patriotic membership organization from the 1890s through the 1960s in Exeter. The "Wehanownwit Tribe No. 22" met weekly, along with the Daughters of Pocahontas, Pekawauket Council No. 36. (EHS)

This group takes some time off, probably at Gilman Park, *c.* 1900. (EHS)

Longtime genealogist Elizabeth Folsom Knowles donated this snapshot of two women, probably Folsom family members around 1900, to the Exeter Historical Society.

Hikers photographed atop Fort Rock, *c.* 1900. Once the property of Ambrose Swasey, this site off Newfields Road was given to the Town of Exeter by the Henderson family. A 1935 guidebook to Exeter mentions a prehistoric fossil shaped like a perfect specimen of a human foot in solid granite nearby. The fossil was known as "Indian Foot."(EHS)

Young boys playing in a field around 1900. (EHS)

Swamscott Lodge, No. 2, of the Knights of Pythias, was instituted in 1870 by the Grand Lodge Officers of Massachusetts. With guiding principles of Friendship, Charity, and Benevolence, they met Monday evenings at the Burlingame Block on Water Street. This photograph dates from around 1907. (TS)

A quintessential cluttered Victorian drawing room photographed around 1900 by an Exeter photographer. (PS)

This unidentified Exeter family posed on the occasion of their matriarch's 90th birthday around 1910, probably for photographer Edwin L. Cunningham. (PEA/ER)

Dr. William H. Nute (1858–1938) was one of Exeter's most beloved physicians. In April 1906, Nute, seen here in his uniform, was elected captain of a state national guard company of sixty-one men in Exeter. A memorial library was named for the doctor during the expansion of the hospital in 1939. (TS)

In 1907 the Higgins family, original proprietors of Higgins Ice Cream Company, gathered in front of their house on Dewey Street. From left to right are: (front row) Ruth, Roger, Al, Paul, and Miles; (middle row) Hattie (later Mrs. Scammon), Frank, Alfred F. with Harold "Tad," John Gray Higgins with George, Harriet (Mrs. John Gray Higgins), Charlie, and George with baby Austin; (back row) Myrtle (Mrs. George Higgins), Abbie (Mrs. Fred Higgins), Charles, Sadie, Dan, Agnes (Mrs. Charles Higgins), Byron, Verna (George's daughter), and Frances (later Mrs. E. Lary). (HH)

Augusta Cenith Beardslee Yeaton (center) operated the trolley waiting station restaurant in the Folsom Tavern with her husband Oliver. Standing behind her on the right is Minnie Yeaton, her daughter-in-law. Clockwise from Minnie in this c. 1913 photograph are: Irma Yeaton Higgins, Minnie's daughter and the owner of Irma's Grill next to the town hall; Marion Gilmore Cooper Dudley, Nellie's daughter; Doris Yeaton McWilliams, Minnie's daughter and the later proprietor of Dot's Flower Shop; and daughter Nellie Yeaton Gilmore (standing). (TS)

The Squamscott Orchestra is shown here around 1908, in a photograph probably by Edwin L. Cunningham. From left to right are: (seated) Alfred Poliquin, Charles Lester Buzell, Perrin Hersey, Charles Higgins (proprietor of Higgins Ice Cream), and James Seward (former drugstore owner); (standing) Howard Brown and Charles Batchelder (late proprietor of Batchelder's Bookstore). (HH)

Edwin L. Cunningham photographed horses and friends around 1910, possibly at his family's farm on Portsmouth Avenue. (EHS)

Young men taking a break from skating on the frozen Exeter River, c. 1915. (EHS)

A parade through "Town Square" moves past the old seasonal bandstand on Front Street, *c.* 1910–16. (PEA)

Local residents gather for a patriotic ceremony, *c.* 1915, in a photograph by Edwin L. Cunningham. (EHS)

Exeter's Third Company, the Coast Artillery Corps of New Hampshire, is shown here in a photograph taken by Edwin L. Cunningham on July 26, 1917. (ENL)

East Kingston farmer Lewie Benson Tilton and his friend Charles W. Young were photographed after a winter hunting trip in the 1920s. Young lived on Linden Street. (EHS)

The Exeter River was the site of this tug of war, *c*. 1920. The champions would remain dry! (PEA/ER)

Participants in the Boy Scout Convention of 1921 pose outside the Congregational Church, in a photograph by the Currier Studio, 187 Water Street. (EHS)

"Mother and Nana" enjoy their new horseless carriage, *c.* 1905. (ENL)

The American Legion basketball team of 1921–22, photographed by Edwin L. Cunningham. From left to right are: (front row) Mr. Glover, Mr Church, Russell H. Welsh, Edward L. Cunningham (the photographer's son in a suit), and Perley Sleeper; (back row) unidentified, Edward Rohr, Mr. Broderic, unidentified, and Frank Welsh. (ENL)

The Exeter Chapter of the DAR, photographed in 1932. The bicentennial year of Washington's birth was commemorated by the chapter with a granite boulder and bronze tablet and the planting of a memorial elm tree at West End Park. This dedication was attended by Mrs. Sarah D. Marston (Exeter DAR Regent from 1931–1933), Dr. Alice Chesley (Honorary State Regent), Mrs. Dorothy M. Nowell, Major James A. Tufts Jr., Albertus T. Dudley, Mrs. Elinor F. Tilton, Miss Margaret McLaughlin, Stephen Winkler, and Miss Elizabeth H. Baker. Young Lorraine Thyng and Crawford Wentworth are pictured in front. (EHS)

This high school reunion in the town hall was photographed by Samuel G. Morse about 1895. (EHS)

Five

School Life

The earliest known photographic image in Exeter is this quarter-plate daguerreotype dated June 1851. From left to right are students in the "Advanced Class at Phillips Exeter Academy": (front row) Nicholas Gilman (died in 1854), Jeremiah Smith (who became a New Hampshire Supreme Court Justice and served on the faculty of Harvard Law School), Theodore E. Colburn (an architect), Charles E. Stetson (a teacher), and Alphonso A. Rice (a civil engineer); (back row) Joseph R. Webster (a doctor), John P. Allison (a banker), David L. Hobbs (a farmer), and Richard A. Barrett (a lawyer). (DW)

Phillips Exeter students assembled for posterity in front of the Second Academy Building in 1865. Phillips Exeter Academy, founded by John Phillips, opened May 1, 1783. This classical building, designed by Ebenezer Clifford and Bradbury Johnson, was constructed in 1794 and destroyed by fire on December 20, 1870. (PEA)

The Third Academy Building was designed by Peabody and Stearns. This structure burned July 4, 1914. Alumni Hall can be seen on the left, and to the right stands the old academy gymnasium. (PEA/ER)

Abbott Hall, room number thirteen, is shown here as it looked when occupied by Herbert O. True and Harlan P. Abbott in 1879. (PEA)

The Nathaniel Weeks House stood on the west side of Court Street, and was removed in 1890 to make room for the Dow House. Pictured are John Heald, Tom Warren, and Cyrus Green, all academy students who rented the property for lodging. (EHS)

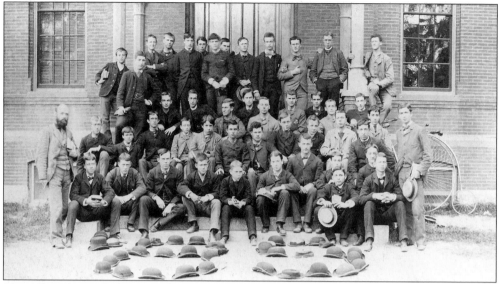

The Class of 1885 from Phillips Exeter Academy, photographed in front of the main academy building. Note the velocipede to the right. (PEA)

Phillips Exeter Academy "gangs" were actually students boarding or eating together at a particular house. In May 1888, the "Chesley Gang" posed outside Chesley House where they "used to eat grub," according to photographer Rob Jones, Class of 1888. (PEA)

Academy students often hammed for the camera, as seen in this "tableau" caught on film around 1889. Pictured in this photograph are: (front row) Mark Ewing (of St. Louis, MO), unidentified, Clarke H. Buford (of Rock Island, IL), and Newton Booth Tarkington (of Indianapolis, IN); (back row) Benjamin S. Cable (of Chicago, IL), Daniel A. Bullard (of Schuylerville, NY), and Elmer R. Holland (of Somerville, MA). (PEA)

Walter W. Metcalf, Class of 1902, wrote "Fraternally Yours" on the reverse of this photograph, c. 1902. Metcalf, an academy student from Westboro, MA, posed with Charles V. Putnam, Class of 1905, from Newport, RI. (PEA)

This was the entire faculty of Phillips Exeter Academy in 1900. (PEA)

The exterior of the chemical and physical laboratories at Phillips Exeter Academy off of Tan Lane, in a photograph taken around 1910. (PEA)

The above image is of the interior of the chemical laboratory, with Burton L. Ely, on January 6, 1900; the image below is of the physics laboratory in 1888. (PEA)

The academy crew was photographed on the Squamscott River by E.L. Cunningham, *c*. 1900. (EHS)

These photographs of the Phillips Exeter Academy crew, original boat house, and scullers were taken by Edwin L. Cunningham around 1900. The building, which once stood at the Exeter River behind the playing fields, no longer remains. (PEA/ER and EHS)

These young members of the Academy Athletic Association, Class of 1892, posed for Exeter photographer Samuel G. Morse. From left to right are: Albert J. Squires (of East Aurora, NY), Thomas T. Thomas (of Boston, MA), John E. Moses (of Exeter), and Vernon K. Irvine (of Bedford, PA). (PEA)

This is the football team of 1889–90 at Phillips Exeter Academy. Notice the lack of padding! (PEA)

A huddle is called at an 1897 football game in Exeter. (PEA)

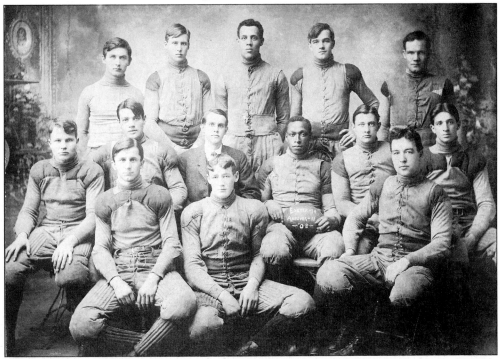

This victory group photograph of the 1903 Phillips Exeter Academy football team was taken by Edwin L. Cunningham. (Note the three point win over rival academy, Phillips Andover.) Cunningham was the academy's official photographer for many years. (PEA)

"Dr. Sauveur's Summer School of Languages" used Phillips Exeter's Third Academy Building (no longer extant). This photograph by Samuel G. Morse is dated 1892. (PEA)

The first school established for girls in Exeter was the Exeter Female Academy in 1826, located on Center Street. The school was superseded by the development of the new female seminary, established through the will of William Robinson in 1865. Robinson charged that the seminary's "course of instruction should be as would tend to make female scholars equal to all the practical duties in life; such a course of education as would enable them to compete, and successfully, too, with their brothers throughout the world, when they take their part in the actual duties of life." Any female resident in town aged nine years or more who was qualified for the grammar school was entitled to receive instruction without the payment of tuition. By 1869 the new school was completed; it was photographed here by Matilda Irvine Hayes, Class of 1889. (ENL)

A biology class at Robinson Female Seminary was photographed c. 1895. The school continued to educate Exeter's young women until 1955. It burned in 1961. The vacant spot where the imposing Second Empire-style structure once stood is located between the rear of Lincoln Street Elementary School and Main Street Elementary School. (ENL)

The Robinson Female Seminary Class of 1899 posed with principal George N. Cross for this class picture. Several instructors are identified including: Elizabeth H. Baker (in the top row holding the cat), who taught geography, U.S. history, and arithmetic from 1890 to 1934; Lillian E. Downes (two down from Mr. Cross, wearing glasses), who taught Latin and Greek from 1895 to 1902; and Clara Esther Kimball (third row from top, second from right), instructor of mathematics and penmanship beginning in 1893. (EHS)

Seventh graders at Court Street School, the town's original high school, pose for the photographer. The school was established in 1848 as a coeducational school, and remained as such until Robinson Female Seminary opened in 1869. These students posed here in 1911 with their teacher, Willard R. Rowe. From left to right are: (front row) unidentified; (second row) William Rowe, Richard Kent, Louis O'Dell, Lester Donovan, LeRoy Junkins, Waldo Hilliard, Philip Brierly, Howard True, Lyman Collishaw, Herbert Boutwell, Chester Scammon, and George Scammon; (third row) Chauncey Mayo, Harold Syphers, Clifton Russell, Richard Litch, Isaac Williams, Ralph Villars, Allen Kreger, and Harry Place; (fourth row) Walter Moss, Arthur Eastman, Lawrence Dunn, Albert Gallant, Spencer Wentworth, Harold Caverly, and ? Philbrick; (back row) Clarence Prescott, Charles Lane, Charles Rand, Mr. Rowe, Harold Perkins, Guy Davis, and Joseph Barlow. (EHS)

The 1922 boys high school basketball team, photographed by Edwin L. Cunningham. Only three members have been able to be identified: Tad Higgins (seated at the front left), Red Hoyt (fourth from left), and Dominic Poggio (standing in the rear at top). (HH)

In 1893, $1,000 was appropriated by voters to build a one-room schoolhouse on Samuel W. Leavitt's land on Winter Street. Forty children enrolled the first year at the school. A new four-room, two-story school building was erected in 1902. Miss Alice Hatch's third grade posed here in September 1907. (EHS)

Spring Street School was established in 1841 as a one-room, ungraded facility, and was one of three brick school buildings in Exeter. Miss Alice Gould's class poses politely here for their photographer, c. 1911. (EHS)

These pupils of Miss Sarah Smith were photographed in 1913. Henry Emery Merrill, age nine, stands in a starched sailor suit with his classmates. Miss Smith ran the small, private elementary school at 36 Court Street. The pupils are, from left to right: (front row) Margaret Kenniston, Frances Smith, Eleanor Perkins, and Lauris Richards; (middle row) Francis Selleck, Walter Carlisle, Marguerite Richmond, Elizabeth Russell, and Richard Perkins; (back row) H. Emery Merrill, Emily R. Dow, Faith Kenniston, and Christine Gillespie. (EHS)

Helen Augusta Yeaton is shown here at about the age of two. Helen was born in 1906 and died in 1912 of diphtheria. Her teacher, Annie Davis, wrote in the *Exeter News-Letter*: "Little Helen. Thursday of last week I watched from the school-house window three small children running merrily to school. Their leader was little Helen Yeaton. This was her last day of school and play. Friday her seat was vacant and Saturday she was in Christ's keeping. Helen was a member of the second grade and ready for promotion to the third, though only six years of age. Seldom has it been my privilege to have a pupil with such a bright, responsive mind. She endeared herself to all who knew her. She will live in our hearts as a pleasant memory of sweet childhood." (TS)

From its earliest days, Exeter was considered a "school town"; its first schoolmaster, Philemon Pormort, began teaching children in the 1640s, and the town's first official schoolhouse was erected around 1707. Conforming with state law a century later, Exeter was divided into six school districts, and grades and a high school were established in 1847. Aside from the Academy, Exeter Female Academy, and Robinson Female Seminary, there were several other schools, including the Emerson School for Boys, St. Michael's School (now Main Street Elementary), and the Exeter Day School. Small elementary schools were located in various neighborhoods during the nineteenth and early twentieth centuries. School Street School, pictured here, was established in 1876, and by 1923 the original one-room building was replaced by a four-room school. This photograph dates from the 1920s.

Acknowledgments

Donations of Exeter photographs and historical materials are strongly encouraged to continue documenting and preserving Exeter's history; contact the Exeter Historical Society, 47 Front Street, PO Box 924, Exeter, NH 03833 (603) 778-2335. All royalties from this publication support the programs of the not-for-profit American Independence Museum, One Governors Lane, Exeter, NH 03833-2422 (603) 772-2622.

The author would like to extend her gratitude to the following organizations and individuals who permitted the use of their historic photographs:
 Exeter Historical Society (EHS)
 Exeter News-Letter, Rockingham County Newspapers (ENL)
 Harold Higgins, North Hampton, NH (HH)
 Phillips Exeter Academy Archives (PEA)
 Phillips Exeter Academy Archives, (PEA/ER); The photograph taken from the archives was printed from a glass plate negative by A.C. Buzzell (1844–1910) or E.L. Cunningham (active 1890–1920), both photographers in Exeter at the turn-of-the-century featured in the "Exeter Remembered—1890–1920" exhibition, 1981.
 Teddie Higgins Smith, Stratham, NH (TS)
 Peter Smith, Exeter, NH (PS); These prints were made from a glass-plate negative taken around 1900–1905 by an unattributed Exeter photographer.
 Dennis A. Waters, Exeter, NH (DW)
 Erin Waters, Exeter, NH (EW)

My heartfelt appreciation is expressed to the following people who helped me discover, identify, research, shared their knowledge and insights, edited my work, or were just plain helpful (or, in the case of Nancy Merrill, all of those things): Ed Chase, Exeter Historical Society; Edouard Desrochers, Phillips Exeter Academy; Dennis A. Waters; budding collector Erin Waters; Harold Higgins; Teddie Smith; Peter Smith; Tom Lynch, Editor, *Exeter News-Letter,* Rockingham County Newspapers; Laura Gowing; Laurie Goff; Valerie Cunningham; Mark Sammons; Erik Tuveson; Allan Cunningham; Matthew Thomas; Ben Swiezynski; Cas Swiezynski, Ben's Foto; Olive Tardiff; Bill Natick; and Bob Tucker, Exeter Public Works Department. Special thanks to Audrey Stomierosky for saving the newspaper archives under her feet; my mother, Thora Irene Stangeland Walker, for dragging me through history (literally!) as a child; Peter Aten for believing working women are a good thing (and tuna melts are a gourmet dinner); Charlie Clark for supporting this project; and Dan Chartrand, Water Street Books, who thought this book *really* should exist.